VIKRAMADITYA'S THRONE

INDRA, KING OF THE GODS, HAD PLEASED SHIVA. AS A REWARD SHIVA GAVE HIM AN EXQUISITE THRONE.

JUST THEN BHARTRIHARI, OUT ON A HUNT, PASSED THAT WAY.

THAT FRUIT! I AM SURE IT'S THE ONE THE BRAHMAN GAVE ME! I'LL TAKE IT FROM HER AND FIND OUT THE TRUTH.

AFTER CONFIRMING THAT IT WAS THE SAME FRUIT, HE SENT FOR ANANGASENA.

TAKE AN OATH THAT YOU WILL ANSWER ME TRUTHFULLY.

I WILL, MY LORD.

WHEN BHARTRIHARI LEARNT THE TRUTH HE WAS UTTERLY DISGUSTED WITH THE WORLD.

THERE IS NO GREATER ENEMY THAN ATTACHMENT, AND NO GREATER HAPPINESS THAN RENUNCIATION.

HE CALLED HIS BROTHER VIKRAMADITYA TO HIM.

I HAVE DECIDED TO BECOME AN ASCETIC. YOU SHALL REIGN IN MY PLACE.

* A GHOST OR DEMON THAT INHABITS CORPSES

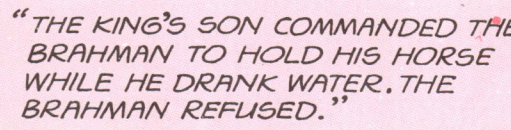

THE MOMENT VIKRAMADITYA SPOKE, THE VETALA DISAPPEARED FROM HIS SHOULDER AND WAS BACK ON THE TREE.

BUT VIKRAMADITYA WENT AFTER HIM AND ONCE AGAIN PLACED HIM ON HIS SHOULDER.

I SHALL TELL YOU ANOTHER STORY. BUT YOU MUST ANSWER MY QUESTION WHEN I FINISH. OR ELSE...

IN THIS WAY THE VETALA TOLD 24 STORIES AND 24 TIMES VIKRAMADITYA BROKE THE SILENCE AND REPLIED. BUT WHEN THE 25TH STORY WAS TOLD VIKRAMADITYA DID NOT KNOW THE ANSWER TO THE GHOUL'S QUESTION AND DID NOT SPEAK A WORD. THE GHOUL WAS FORCED TO STAY ON HIS SHOULDER AND COULD NOT ESCAPE BACK TO HIS TREE.

THIS KING IS COURAGEOUS, CLEVER AND COMPASSIONATE. I MUST WARN HIM OF THE SORCERER.

O KING, THE SORCERER INTENDS TO KILL YOU.

INDRA GAVE PRESENTS TO VIKRAMADITYA. AMONG THEM WAS SHIVA'S THRONE.

THIS THRONE TOO IS YOURS, GREAT KING. IT WAS GIVEN TO ME BY LORD SHIVA.

TAKING LEAVE OF INDRA, VIKRAMADITYA RETURNED TO UJJAINI WITH ALL HIS GIFTS. THERE HE SET UP THE THRONE AND ON AN AUSPICIOUS DAY MOUNTED IT.

FROM THE DAY HE MOUNTED THE THRONE, HIS RULE WAS GLORIOUS IN EVERY WAY. HE WAS THE OVERLORD OF ALL THE KINGS ON EARTH. HE VANQUISHED ALL EVIL MEN. POVERTY WAS UNKNOWN AND FAMINE AND GRIEF UNHEARD OF. SAVANTS AND SCHOLARS PROSPERED UNDER HIS PATRONAGE.

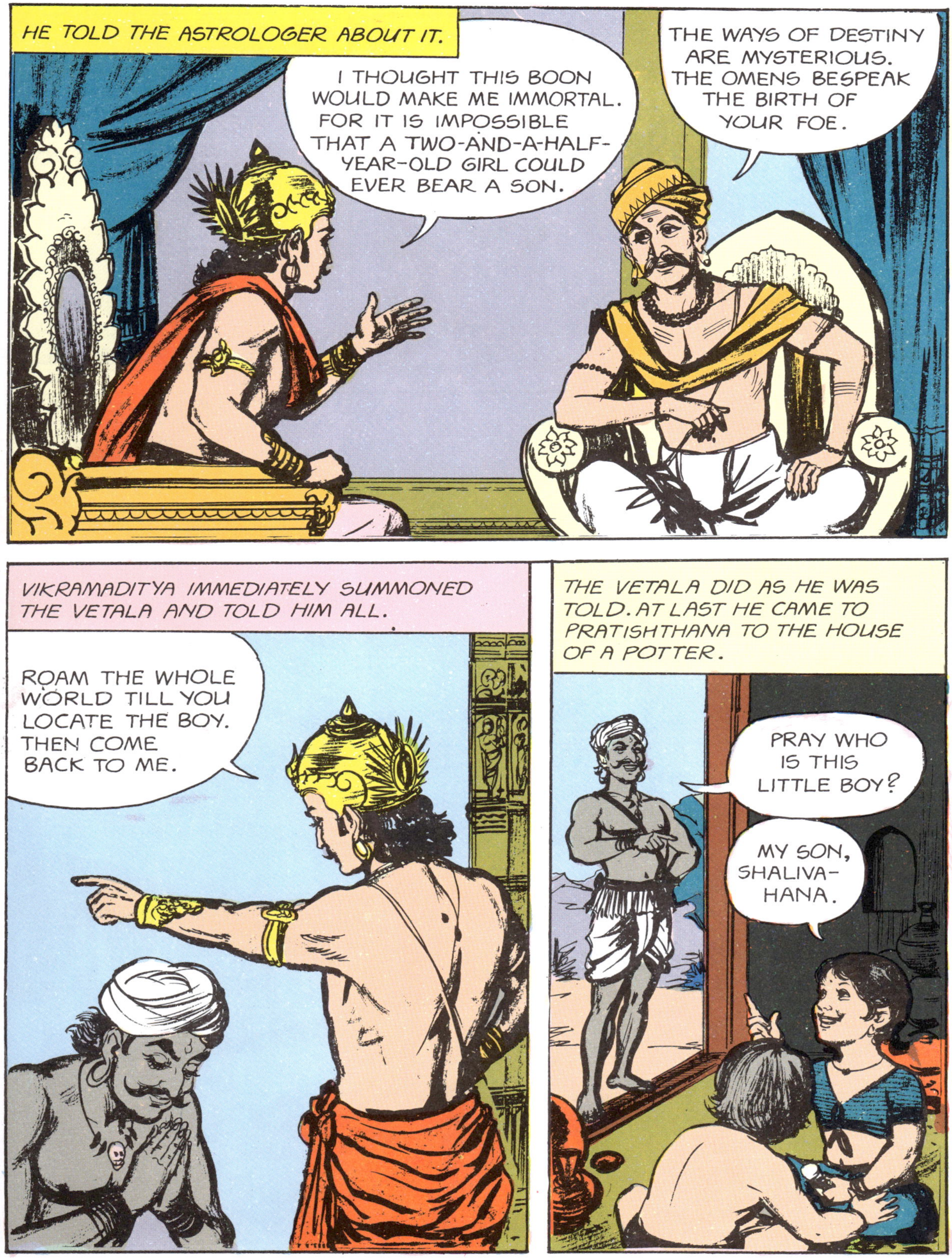

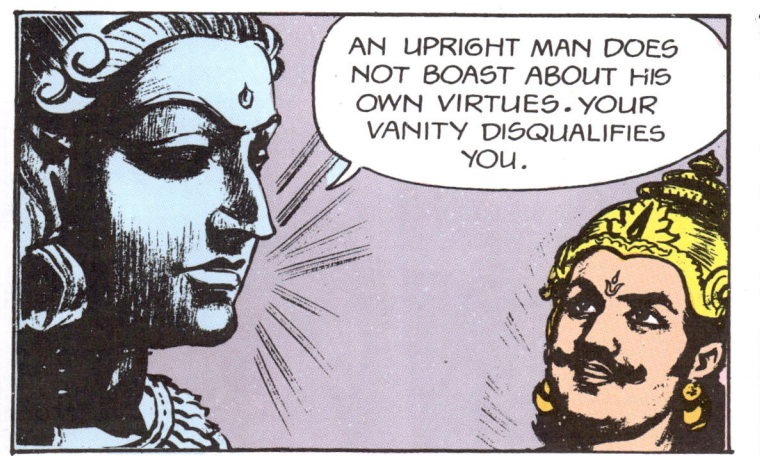

"YES. LET THE ADVENTURES OF VIKRAMADITYA BECOME IMMORTAL UPON EARTH. LET ALL WHO HEAR THEM BE SAFE FROM ANY DANGER."

"SO BE IT."

RAJA BHOJA PLACED THE THRONE IN A SHRINE INLAID WITH BRIGHT GOLD AND THE NINE PRECIOUS GEMS. UPON IT HE PLACED THE IMAGES OF SHIVA AND PARVATI AND WORSHIPPED BOTH, THE THRONE AND THE DEITIES.

THEN MOUNTING THE THRONE HE RULED WISELY AND WELL TILL THE END OF HIS DAYS.

9 amazing offers on your favourite reads!

Get additional 20% off on ACK Complete Collection.
Code: ACKCC20
www.amarchitrakatha.com

Get additional 15% off on any ACK Complete Collection Volumes (1, 2 & 3).
Code: ACKV15
www.amarchitrakatha.com

Get flat 15% off on all India Book House books on amarchitrakatha.com.
Code: IBHACK15
www.amarchitrakatha.com

Get additional 20% off on 1 year Subscription of Tinkle magazine
Code: TINKLE20
www.amarchitrakatha.com

Get additional 25% off on 1 year Subscription of Tinkle Combo
Code: ACKTC25
www.amarchitrakatha.com

Get additional 10% off on 1 year Subscription of Brainwave
Code: BRAINWAVE10
www.amarchitrakatha.com

Get flat 30% discount on all Karadi Products on Amarchitrakatha.com.
Code: KARADI30
www.amarchitrakatha.com

Get additional 15% off on 1 year Subscription of Nationa Geographic
Code: NATGEO15
getnationalgeographic.com

Get additional 5% off on 1 year Subscription of National Geographic Magazine and National Geographic Traveller India Combo
Code: NGC05
getnationalgeographic.com

How to Redeem:
1. Log on to www.amarchitrakatha.com for Amar Chitra Katha offers and www.getnationalgeographic.com for National Geographic offers
2. Select the products you wish to buy and add to your shopping cart.
3. Proceed to "Checkout & Pay" and enter the coupon code in discount Code section. Click on the "Verify" button & proceed with the address and payments details.

Terms and Conditions:
1. Customers can redeem the coupon code only at our online stores.
2. To avail the discount, customer will have to submit the coupon code at the checkout page.
3. ACK Media reserves the right to change or withdraw the offer and/or the promo codes, anytime, at the sole discretion of the management.
4. All standard Terms & Conditions available at amarchitrakatha.com & getnationalgeographic.com will apply.